JANUARY

# On the fourth day of creation, God created the sun, moon and stars.

Two of the stars are different from the rest.
Can you spot them?
You can find the story of creation in your Bible in
Genesis 1.

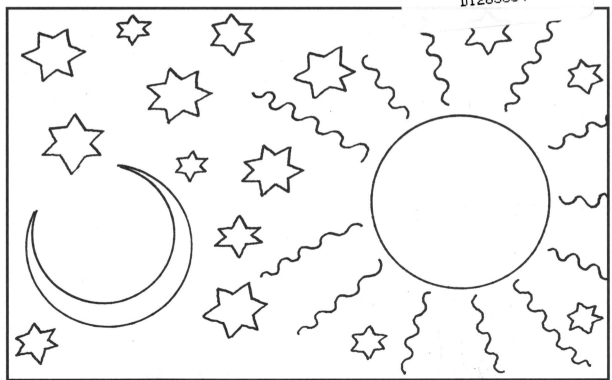

On the fifth day of creation, God created the fish of the sea and the birds of the air.

**Which outline matches exactly the complete fish?**
**Now complete the picture by adding some sea creatures.**
**You can find this story in Genesis 1:20–23.**

JANUARY

Puzzle

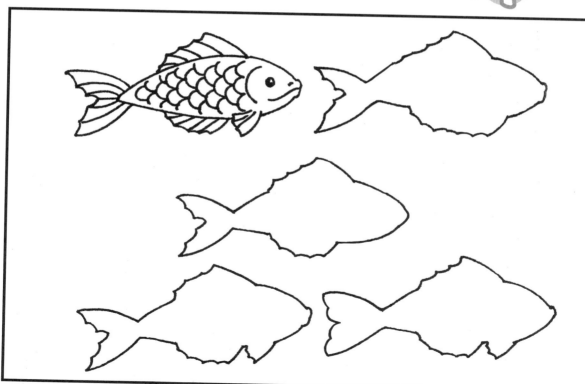

# 31
### DECEMBER

It's the last day of the year! We remember the last year and look forward to the next.

Do you remember the story the artist has drawn here?
Read the story in John 6:1-13.
Now number the pictures in the right order.
Write down what you hope for in the new year.

# 3

## JANUARY

God now created the first man, Adam, and the first woman, Eve, to live in the Garden of Eden.

**Spot all the differences between these two pictures of Eden. You can find the story of Adam and Eve in Genesis 2:7–25.**

SPOT THE DIFFERENCE

# 30

## DECEMBER

Here are 6 pictures of the Christmas story.

**Can you number them in the right order?**
**Look in Luke 2 and Matthew 2 to help you.**

*Puzzle*

# 4

JANUARY

Adam named all the animals and birds.

**Complete the outline drawings of the animals.
You can read this story in your Bible in
Genesis 2:19–20.**

**Draw me!**

**29**

DECEMBER

Mary and Joseph took baby Jesus to the Temple to thank God for him. An old man called Simeon held the baby. He too thanked God.

**Join up the dots to complete the picture.**
**Read Luke 2:25–32.**

DOT-TO-DOT

# 5

JANUARY

Here are some of the birds named by Adam.

**Copy the drawing into the blank box and then color your new picture. Read Genesis 2:19–20.**

**Draw me!**

**28**

DECEMBER

The wise men brought gifts to Jesus. What were they?

**Read Matthew 2:11 to find out.**
**Now join up the wise men with their presents.**

*maze*

**JANUARY**

God told Adam and Eve not to eat the fruit from this tree.

**What hidden objects can you find in the picture of the tree in the Garden of Eden?**
**You can read what God said in Genesis 3:2.**

Search

# 27

## DECEMBER

Here are the wise men visiting Jesus.

How many mistakes can you find in the picture?
Read Matthew 2:11.

SPOT THE MISTAKE

**7**

**JANUARY**

What creature is going to trick Eve into doing wrong?

You can find this story in Genesis 3:1–7.
Can you find the mistakes in the picture?

SPOT THE MISTAKE

# 26
## DECEMBER

The wise men were filled with joy when they saw the star again and it led them to Bethlehem.

**Which outline star exactly fits the finished star?**
**Read Matthew 2:9–10.**

*Puzzle*

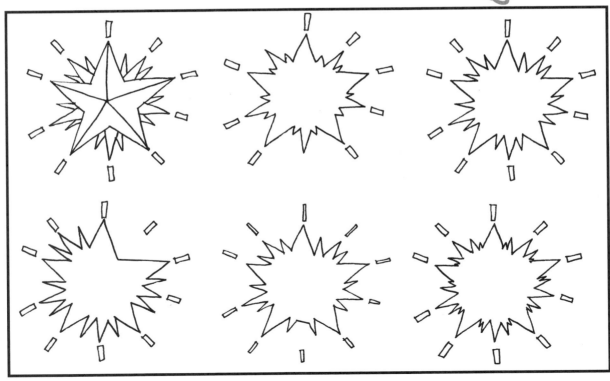

**8**

JANUARY

Puzzle

The snake made up lies about God.

**Which 2 snakes in this picture are exactly the same?**
**How is the snake described in Genesis 3:1?**

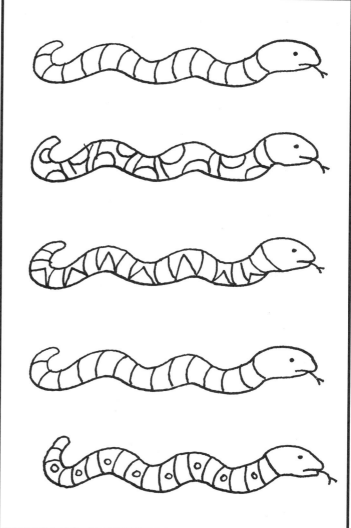

### Christmas Day
Here is the Christmas star shining clearly above the little town of Bethlehem.

**Copy this picture neatly into the blank box.**
**Read Matthew 2:9.**

**Draw me!**

# 9
## JANUARY

Here are Adam and Eve at the tree.
What do you think they are saying?

**Look in your Bible at Genesis 3:6 and fill in the speech bubbles.**

*Talk to me!*

**24**

DECEMBER

When the wise men arrived in Jerusalem, they asked King Herod where they might find the new-born king.

You can read this story in Matthew 2:1–8.
Now copy the drawing and color it in.

**Draw me!**

**10**

JANUARY

DOT-TO-DOT

God expelled Adam
and Eve from Eden.
Who did he use to
keep them out?

**Join up the dots to find out.**
**Now color in the picture.**
**Read about this in Genesis 3:21–24.**

**23**

**DECEMBER**

In the East, wise men were watching the skies. They saw a new star. "A new king has been born," they said.

You can read this story in Matthew 2:1–2.
Help the wise men find the way across the desert.

*maze*

JANUARY

Adam and Eve are leaving Eden for a barren place.

**Help Adam and Eve find their way from Eden to the dry desert. You can read this story in Genesis 3:21–24.**

maze

**22**

**DECEMBER**

The shepherds went to the stable in Bethlehem to see the baby Jesus. They told Mary what the angels had said.

**You can read this story in Luke 2:15–20.**
**Join up the dots to complete the picture.**

DOT-TO-DOT

# 12

## JANUARY

Adam and Eve's son Cain attacked his brother Abel.

**Find the deliberate mistakes in this picture.**
**You can find out what happened to the two brothers in Genesis 4:1–16.**

SPOT THE MISTAKE

In fields near Bethlehem, shepherds were looking after their sheep. What happened next?

**Read Luke 2:8–14 to find out.**
**Can you find all the crowns hidden here?**

Search

JANUARY

DOT-TO-DOT

God told Noah to build a big boat.

**The artist hasn't finished this picture of Noah's Ark.**
**Complete the picture – then color it in.**
**Read Genesis 6:9–16.**

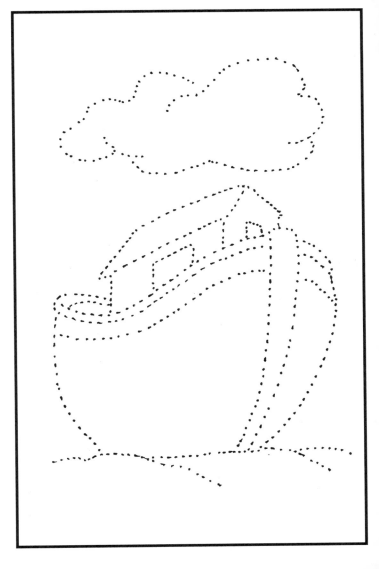

# 20
## DECEMBER

When Joseph and Mary arrived in Bethlehem, they found that there was no room for them at the inn.

**You can read about this in Luke 2:7.**
**Complete this picture of the stable where Jesus was born by drawing some animals.**

**Draw me!**

# 14

## JANUARY

God told Noah to collect together 2 of every kind of animal.

Spot the odd one out in this picture of the animals waiting to enter the ark.
Look in Genesis 6:21 to find out what God also told Noah to put in the ark.

Puzzle

# 19

DECEMBER

Joseph and Mary had to travel to Bethlehem to register their names.

**You can read about this in Luke 2:4–5.**
**Help Joseph and Mary find their way to Bethlehem through the maze of roads.**

maze

**15**

JANUARY

Noah's wife, his three sons and their wives also went into the ark.

Copy into the blank box this picture of the animals marching into the ark two by two.

Now color your picture in.

Read Genesis 6:10 to find the names of Noah's sons.

**Draw me!**

**18**

**DECEMBER**

Here is Mary with her cousin Elizabeth, who was also expecting a baby. Do you remember what his name was to be?

**Read Luke 1:60 to find the answer.**
**Color in the picture neatly.**

Color me!

# 16

## JANUARY

God told Noah to make small rooms in the ark.

**These 3 animals have lost their partners.**
**Follow the lines and draw in each missing animal.**
**Read Genesis 7:14.**

maze

# 17
## DECEMBER

We are getting very near Christmas! For the last days of December, we'll look again at the story of Christmas.

Here's the angel telling Mary she will have a special baby. Can you find the silly mistakes that the artist has made? Read Luke 1:26–38.

SPOT THE MISTAKE

# 17

## JANUARY

Everyone is now safely aboard the ark.

**Can you find the deliberate mistakes in this picture?**
**Read Genesis 7:13–20.**

SPOT THE MISTAKE

# 16

## DECEMBER

Here are some pictures from Paul's life. Can you put them in the right order?

**Number them from 1–6.**
**Look in Acts 9 – 27 to help you.**

Puzzle

**18**

JANUARY

The flood has begun and the ark is adrift on the water.

Complete this drawing, adding rain and lightning, waves and spray.
Read Genesis 7:17–20.

**Draw me!**

# 15

## DECEMBER

Paul spent the last years of his life in a prison in Rome. But he kept writing letters to his friends everywhere.

**Join up the dots to finish the picture.**
**What did Paul ask Timothy to bring him in prison?**
**Read 2 Timothy 4:13 to find out.**

DOT-TO-DOT

**19**

JANUARY

The rain stopped after 40 days. But the floodwaters took a very long time to go down.

**Read Genesis 8:11.**
**What did the dove bring back in its beak?**
**Which outline matches the finished bird?**

Puzzle

# 14

## DECEMBER

Paul and his friend Silas were put in prison for preaching the gospel.

**Finish drawing the prison cell.**
**Where is the door?**
**Are there bars at the windows?**
**Read Acts 16:22–23.**

**Draw me!**

# 20

## JANUARY

Noah sent out another bird as well as the dove. Which bird?

**Read Genesis 8:6–9 to find out.**
**Which outline exactly matches the finished picture?**

Puzzle

# 13

DECEMBER

In Jerusalem an angry mob tried to kill Paul. Roman soldiers rescued him, then put him in prison.

**Finish this picture by drawing Paul surrounded by some more soldiers. Read Acts 21:30–36.**

**Draw me!**

JANUARY

DOT-TO-DOT

Noah, his family and all the animals finally leave the ark.

**Join up the dots to complete the picture. Now color it in. Read Genesis 8:15–19.**

# 12
## DECEMBER

Paul went to the famous city
of Athens to preach.

**How many funny mistakes can you find here?**
**Read Acts 17:16 to find out what made Paul feel sad in Athens.**

SPOT THE MISTAKE

**22**

JANUARY

When Noah, his family and all the animals finally left the ark, God sent a sign and promised never to flood the world again.

**Find the differences between these pictures.**
**What was God's sign?**
**Read Genesis 9:12–17 to find out.**

SPOT THE DIFFERENCE

# 11

## DECEMBER

Aquila and Priscilla were tent-makers.

Copy this picture into the empty space and then color it in neatly.
Read Acts 18:1–4.

**Draw me!**

# 23

JANUARY

Here are 6 pictures telling the story of Noah. Number them in the right order.

You can read the whole story in Genesis 6:1 – 9:17.

*Puzzle*

# 10

## DECEMBER

Paul traveled from town to town telling everyone the good news about Jesus.

**Join up the dots to find out what's happening here.**
**Read the story of Paul and his friends in Acts 18:1–4, 18–23.**
**What did they all do for a job?**

DOT-TO-DOT

**24**

JANUARY

After Noah's time, some people started building a huge tower that would reach the sky.

Complete the picture so that the tower is much higher and builders are busy on it. Read Genesis 11:1–4.

**Draw me!**

# 9

Paul escaped from Damascus in a basket.

**Which outline fits the finished basket?**
**Read Acts 9:19b–25.**

Puzzle

## 25

### Puzzle

The builders used shovels, mud bricks and tar to build the Tower of Babel.

**Which 2 hammers are exactly the same? Read Genesis 11:3–4.**

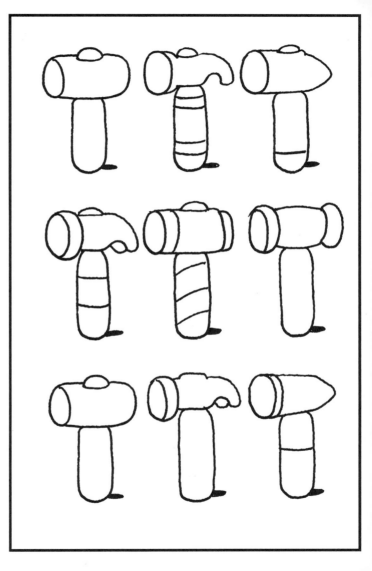

# 8

## DECEMBER

After Jesus spoke to him, Paul became a Christian himself.

**Join up the dots to find out how he escaped his enemies in Damascus. Read Acts 9:19b–25.**

DOT-TO-DOT

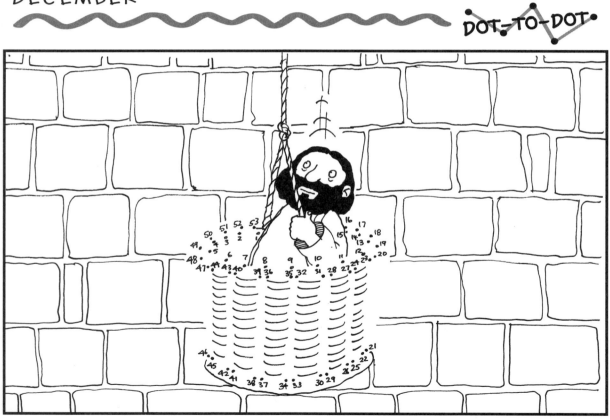

## 26

JANUARY

God called Abram to travel from his home in Ur to the Promised Land.

**Find the mistakes in this picture of Abram traveling to the Promised Land.**
**Read Genesis 11:31–32 and 12:1–8.**

SPOT THE MISTAKE

# 7

## DECEMBER

Paul traveled to Damascus to harm the Christians living there. On the way, Jesus spoke to him.

**Read the whole story in Acts 9:1–18.**
**Can you find the differences between these pictures of Paul being stopped on his journey?**

SPOT THE DIFFERENCE

# 27

## JANUARY

Abram's wife, Sarai, and his nephew, Lot, went with him.

**Help Abram find the right way from Ur to the Promised Land.**
**Read Genesis 11:31–32 and 12:1–8.**

maze

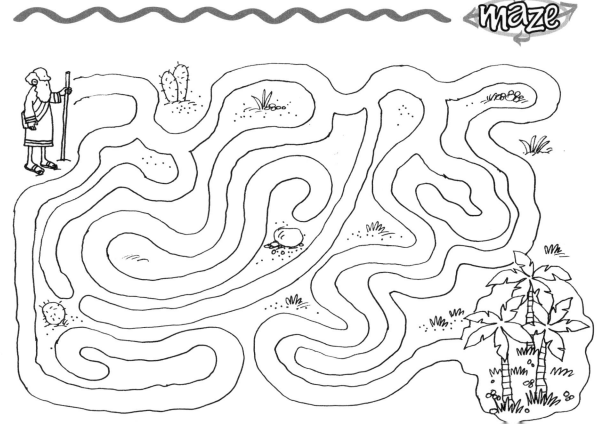

**6**

DECEMBER

Philip met a man riding a chariot who wanted to understand his Bible. Philip told him about Jesus.

**Can you find all the flowers hidden in this picture?**
**Read Acts 8:26–40.**

Search 👉

**28**

JANUARY

Abram and Lot went their separate ways some time after they arrived in the Promised Land.

**How many jugs can you find hidden here?**
**Read Genesis 13:1–18.**

Search

# 5

## DECEMBER

Peter went to visit a Roman soldier called Cornelius.

**Can you help Peter find the way? Read the story of what happened in Acts 10:23–48.**

**29**

JANUARY

God told Abraham to count the stars. Find out why in Genesis 15:5.

**Can you find Sarah hidden in the picture? Read Genesis 17:5–6 and 17:15–16 to find out why God changed Abram's and Sarai's names.**

Search

# 4

## DECEMBER

Peter is preaching to a crowd of people in Jerusalem.

**Can you find the deliberate mistakes the artist has made?**
**Read Acts 5:29 to find out what Peter said**
**when he was told to stop preaching.**

SPOT THE MISTAKE

# 30

JANUARY

Three special messengers are visiting Abraham and Sarah. Join up the dots to see them properly.

**You can read the story of Abraham's visitors and their message in Genesis 18:1–15. Who were the messengers?**

DOT-TO-DOT

**3**

DECEMBER

Here are two pictures of Dr Luke,
who wrote the Gospel of Luke
and the Book of Acts.

How many differences can you find between the two pictures?
Read Luke 1:1–4 to find out why Luke wrote his books.

SPOT THE DIFFERENCE

## 31

JANUARY

## Color me!

Abraham's wife Sarah was very old. She laughed when she heard the visitor say she would have a baby son.

**Color in this picture of Abraham, Sarah and baby Isaac.**
**Read this story in Genesis 18:1–15 and 21:1–3.**

# 2
## DECEMBER

An angel came to rescue
Peter from prison.

**Can you find 10 little bowls hidden in the picture?
Read the whole story in Acts 12:1–18.**

Search

**FEBRUARY**

God tested Abraham, telling him to sacrifice Isaac.

**Find the deliberate mistakes in this picture.**
**You can read this story in Genesis 22:1–19.**
**Was Isaac safe?**

SPOT THE MISTAKE

# DECEMBER

Peter cured a man who was crippled.

**Join up the dots to find out what Peter is doing here.**
**Read the story in Acts 3:1–8.**
**Where did Peter find the crippled man?**

DOT-TO-DOT

**2**

FEBRUARY

Abraham sent his servant to find a wife for Isaac. The servant found Rebekah when she came to the well.

**How did Isaac feel when he met Rebekah?**
**You can find out in Genesis 24:61–67.**
**How many jars can you find hidden in the picture?**

Search

# 30

## NOVEMBER

After Pentecost, Peter and the other disciples preached boldly in Jerusalem.

**Copy the picture of Peter.**
**Read Acts 2:41 to see how many people became Christians as a result of Peter's sermon.**

**Draw me!**

**3**

**FEBRUARY**

Many years later, Isaac and Rebekah had twin sons, named Jacob and Esau.

**Can you find all the rattles hidden in the drawing?**
**Read Genesis 25:19–26.**

Search 👉

# 29
## NOVEMBER

On the day of Pentecost, tongues of fire appeared on the disciples' heads.

**Which group of disciples is the odd one out?**
**Read about the Day of Pentecost in Acts 2:1–4.**

Puzzle

**4**

Here are Abraham, his son Isaac, and his grandson Jacob.

**Follow the lines to connect them up to their wives. Then color in all the family.**

maze

Abraham and Sarah

Isaac and Rebekah

Jacob and Rachel

**28**

NOVEMBER

After 40 days, Jesus went back to heaven.

**Color in the picture of him ascending to heaven. Read Luke 24:50–53.**

Color me!

**5**

FEBRUARY

Jacob deceived his father by pretending to be his older brother, Esau. He put goats' skin on his arms to pretend he was hairy.

**Can you find Esau hidden in this picture?**
**Read Genesis 27:1–35.**

Search

# 27

## NOVEMBER

### What is the risen Lord Jesus doing here?

**Read John 21:1–14 to find out.**
**Can you find all the funny mistakes the artist has made?**

SPOT THE MISTAKE

## FEBRUARY

### maze

Jacob had to run away to his uncle Laban who lived in Haran.

**Can you help Jacob find the right path? Read Genesis 27:41–44.**

# 26

NOVEMBER

After Jesus rose from the dead, he appeared to his disciples when they were in a locked room.

**Can you find 10 keys hidden here?**
**Read John 20:19–20.**

Search 👉

**7**

**FEBRUARY**

On his way, Jacob slept in the open. One night he dreamt of angels going up and down a stairway to heaven.

**Which angel is different from the rest?**
**Read Genesis 28:10–17.**

SPOT THE DIFFERENCE

**25**

NOVEMBER

Two of Jesus' friends were walking sadly to the village of Emmaus.

You can read about this in Luke 24:13–35.
Add to the picture someone else who walked with them. Who is it?

**Draw me!**

**8**

FEBRUARY

When he was in Haran, Jacob married his uncle's daughter, Rachel.

**Finish this picture by drawing Jacob next to his new wife. You can find this story in Genesis 29:1–30.**

**Draw me!**

Mary was very sad when she saw that Jesus' tomb was empty.

**Join up the dots to discover what she saw next.**
**Read the whole story in John 20:10–18.**

DOT-TO-DOT

# 9

FEBRUARY

While Jacob was traveling back to meet Esau again, he wrestled with an angel in the desert.

**How many deliberate mistakes can you find?**
**Read Genesis 32:22–31.**

SPOT THE MISTAKE

# 23

NOVEMBER

Jesus' friends, Peter and John, ran to the tomb. They found it was empty. Jesus had risen from the dead!

**You can read about this in John 20:1–9.**
**Can you find all the candles hidden here?**

Search 👉

# 10

**FEBRUARY**

After many years, Jacob and Esau meet again. Esau forgives Jacob for deceiving his father.

**Color in this picture of the twin brothers meeting. See Genesis 33:1–16.**

Color me!

# 22

**NOVEMBER**

After Jesus died on the cross, he was buried in a cave. When some women visited his tomb they found it was empty.

**Can you find the differences between the 2 pictures?**
**Read this story in Luke 24:1–12.**
**Who spoke to the women?**

SPOT THE DIFFERENCE

**FEBRUARY**

Jacob had many sons – but Joseph was his favorite. Here Joseph is dreaming about bundles of wheat.

**Which two bundles are exactly the same?**
**Read Genesis 37:3–8.**

*Puzzle*

# 21
## NOVEMBER

Judas was paid 30 silver coins to betray Jesus. What is he doing with the money here?

**Read the story in Matthew 27:1–10.**
**Can you find all the deliberate mistakes here?**

SPOT THE MISTAKE

# 12

## FEBRUARY

## What is Joseph wearing here?

**Join the dots to find out.**
**Read Genesis 37:3–4.**

DOT-TO-DOT

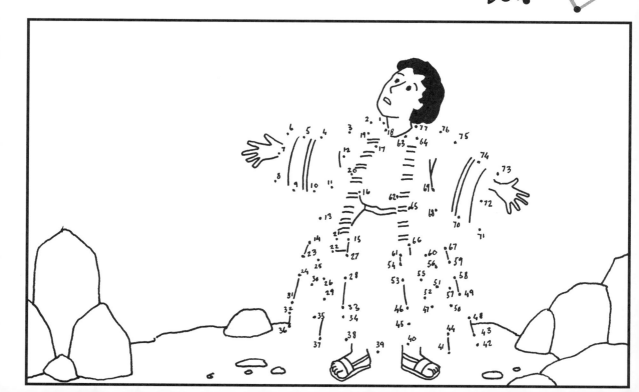

# 20
## NOVEMBER

Here are 6 pictures of the story of Jesus' death on the cross.

Can you number them in the right order?
Look in Matthew 26 and 27 to help you.
Read Mark 15:27 to find out who the men were who were crucified on each side of Jesus.

Puzzle

## FEBRUARY

Jacob gave his favorite son a very special coat.

**How many mistakes has the artist made in this picture?**
**Read Genesis 37:3–4.**

The soldiers took Jesus to a place called the Skull and killed him on a cross.

**You can read about this in Luke 23:33–34.**
**What is Jesus saying?**
**Write the words in his speech bubble.**

*Talk to me!*

# 14

FEBRUARY

Joseph's brothers are selling Joseph to traveling merchants called Midianites.

**How many bags of money can you find hidden in the picture? You can read this story in Genesis 37:12–28.**

Search

**18**

NOVEMBER

Here's a Roman soldier's helmet.

Copy it into the blank box and color it in.

**Draw me!**

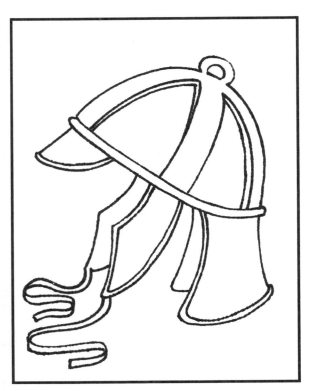

# 15

**FEBRUARY**

The merchants are taking Joseph across the desert to Egypt.

**Help this Midianite find the right path to Egypt.**
**Read Genesis 37:12–28.**

maze

# 17

## NOVEMBER

Roman soldiers treated Jesus very badly.

**Which of these 4 soldiers is the odd man out?**
**Read Matthew 27:27–31 to see what the soldiers did.**

SPOT THE DIFFERENCE

# 16

## FEBRUARY

In Egypt, Joseph worked for an army captain called Potiphar.

**Can you find any deliberate mistakes in this picture of Joseph and Potiphar's wife?**
**Read Genesis 39:1–5.**

SPOT THE MISTAKE

# 16
## NOVEMBER

Pontius Pilate washed his hands to show he didn't want to take the blame for having Jesus put to death on the cross.

**Read Matthew 27:24–26.**
**Now fill in Pilate's speech bubble.**

*Talk to me!*

# 17

## FEBRUARY

Joseph was thrown into prison although he hadn't done anything wrong.

**Who else was put in prison with Joseph?**
**Read Genesis 39:19 – 40:3 to find out.**
**Now complete the picture and color it in.**

**Draw me!**

# 15

## NOVEMBER

Jesus was taken before the Roman ruler, called Pontius Pilate.

**The artist has missed out the most important figure.**
**Read this story in Matthew 27:11–26**
**and then add the other person.**

**Draw me!**

**18**

FEBRUARY

In prison Pharaoh's baker had a dream about bread and the butler had a dream about grapes.

**Follow the lines to find out who is the butler and who is the baker.**
**Read Genesis 40:5–23.**

maze

**14**

NOVEMBER

Peter swore he didn't know Jesus.
Then he heard the rooster crow.

**Can you find the differences between the two pictures?
Read Mark 14:71–72.**

SPOT THE DIFFERENCE

# 19

## FEBRUARY

Joseph was brought out of prison to explain Pharaoh's dreams.

**Join up the dots to find one of the dreams.**
**Read Genesis 41:1–14.**

**13**

NOVEMBER

Peter crept into the courtyard of the high priest's house. He was very frightened.

**Can you find the roosters' heads hidden in the picture? Read Mark 14:66–70.**

Search 👉

**20**

FEBRUARY

Joseph is explaining the dreams to Pharaoh.

Write what Joseph is saying in the bubble.
Read Genesis 41:15–32 to help you.

*Talk to me!*

# 12

**NOVEMBER**

After Jesus was arrested, he was taken before the Jewish high priest, who was called Caiaphas.

**Add Jesus to the picture – and Peter trying to hide. Now color it in. You can read about this in Matthew 26:57–58.**

**Draw me!**

# 21
## FEBRUARY

## Puzzle

Pharaoh asked Joseph to build storehouses and store up grain for when the famine came.

**Which storehouse is the odd one out? Why?**

**Read this story in Genesis 41:46–49.**

**NOVEMBER**

The guards arrested Jesus in the Garden of Gethsemane.

Color in the picture.
You can read this story in Matthew 26:47–56.

Color me!

# 22

## FEBRUARY

One day, because there was no food where they lived, Joseph's brothers came to Egypt to buy grain.

**Color in this picture of the brothers meeting Joseph again. Why are they bowing down? Read Genesis 42:1–8.**

Color me!

# 10
## NOVEMBER

While Jesus prayed, all his disciples fell asleep in the garden.

**Can you find the deliberate mistakes in this picture? Read Mathew 26:40–45.**

SPOT THE MISTAKE

FEBRUARY

# The brothers took sacks of grain back home.

**Which 2 sacks are exactly the same?**
**Read Genesis 42:25–38.**

Puzzle

# 9

## NOVEMBER

Jesus went at night to the Garden of Gethsemane.

**Join up the dots to see what he is doing there.**
**Read this story in Matthew 26:36–39.**

DOT-TO-DOT

# 24

**FEBRUARY**

The brothers went to Egypt again. On the way home they found a silver cup in the youngest brother's sack.

**How many differences can you find between these 2 pictures? Read Genesis 44:1–13. What's the name of the youngest brother?**

SPOT THE DIFFERENCE

**8**

NOVEMBER

Here is a picture of some of Jesus' friends eating and drinking at the Last Supper.

Copy the picture into the blank box and color it in.
Read about the Last Supper in Matthew 26:17–30.

**Draw me!**

# 25

## FEBRUARY

Joseph saw that the brothers
were now loving and kind.
So he told them who he was.

**How many silly mistakes can you see here?**
**Read Genesis 45:1–15.**

SPOT THE MISTAKE

**7**

NOVEMBER

During the meal, Jesus washed his friends' feet.

**Complete the picture by drawing Peter having his feet washed. Read John 13:1–17.**

**Draw me!**

# 26

## FEBRUARY

The artist has drawn pictures of different events in Joseph's life. Can you number them in the right order?

**Look in Genesis 37 – 45 to help you.**

*Puzzle*

NOVEMBER

Search 👉

Jesus had a special supper with his 12 disciples in an upper room in Jerusalem. Jesus broke the bread for them.

**Can you find all the loaves hidden here? Read about this in Matthew 26:26.**

**27**

FEBRUARY

Finally Jacob came to Egypt to see his favorite son again.

**Read Genesis 45:25–28 and 46:28–29.**
**Now color in the picture.**

Color me!

# 5

## NOVEMBER

The priests gave Judas 30 silver coins to tell them where they could find Jesus.

**Can you find the funny mistakes here?**
**Read Luke 22:1–6.**

SPOT THE MISTAKE

**28**

FEBRUARY

Many years later, Joseph's descendants were still in Egypt. But they were forced to work as slaves.

Complete this picture of a slave helping to build one of Pharaoh's palaces.
Read Exodus 1:8–14.

**Draw me!**

**4**

NOVEMBER

## What is Jesus doing in the market at the Jerusalem Temple?

How many differences can you discover between the two pictures?
You can read the whole story in Mark 11:15–17.

SPOT THE DIFFERENCE

**MARCH**

When he was a baby, Moses' mother hid him among the reeds in the River Nile.

Join up the dots to find what Moses' mother put him in. You can read the story of baby Moses in Exodus 2:1–10.

DOT-TO-DOT

**3**

NOVEMBER

**Search** 👉

As Jesus rode on the donkey into Jerusalem, people waved palm branches.

**How many palm branches can you find hidden here?**
**Read what happened in Matthew 21:8–11.**

## MARCH

### Puzzle

The ducks in the Nile are surprised to see baby Moses in a basket.

**Which 2 ducks are exactly the same?**
**Read Exodus 2:1–4.**
**Who is watching baby Moses to keep him safe?**

**2**

NOVEMBER

Jesus told his friends to borrow a donkey for him to ride into the city of Jerusalem.

**Which outline fits the finished donkey?**
**Complete all the donkeys.**
**You can read this story in Matthew 21:1–7.**

Puzzle

**3**

MARCH

One of Pharaoh's daughters spotted the basket in the reeds.

**What is the princess saying in this picture of Moses in the basket by the Nile? Fill in her speech bubble.**
**Read Exodus 2:5–6 to help you.**
**Now color in the picture.**

*Talk to me!*

**NOVEMBER**

Jesus' friend Lazarus died
and was laid in a tomb.
What happened next?

**Join up the dots to find out.**
**Read John 11:1–44.**

DOT-TO-DOT

**4**

MARCH

The princess paid Moses' mother to look after baby Moses. When he was older, he grew up as a royal prince.

**How many frogs can you find hidden here?**
**Read Exodus 2:7–10.**

Search

## 31

OCTOBER

**Search** 👉

Mary and Martha sometimes looked after Jesus in their house in Bethany.

**Can you find all the objects hidden here? Read this story in Luke 10:38–42.**

## 5

**MARCH**

SPOT THE DIFFERENCE

Even in the time of Moses, there were old pyramids in Egypt.

**Can you spot the odd one out?**

# 30

OCTOBER

This woman was very poor — but she gave God what she could.

Can you find 10 coins hidden in the picture? Read what Jesus says about this poor widow in Luke 21:1–4.

Search

**6**

MARCH

Which of these outlines fits completely the finished drawing of Egyptian pyramids?

*Puzzle*

**29**
OCTOBER

Here is another picture of
the man thanking Jesus.
The others are rejoicing.

**Read the story in Luke 17:11–19
and fill in Jesus' speech bubble.**

*Talk to me!*

**7**

MARCH

One day, when Moses grew up, he saw an Egyptian punishing a Hebrew slave. Moses was so angry that he hit the Egyptian.

How many differences can you spot between the two pictures? You can read this story in Exodus 2:11–15.

SPOT THE DIFFERENCE

**28**

OCTOBER

SPOT THE MISTAKE

Jesus healed 10 men —
but only one said
"Thank you."

**Find all the mistakes in this picture of the healed man thanking Jesus. Read this story in Luke 17:11–19.**

**8**

MARCH

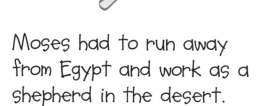

SPOT THE MISTAKE

Moses had to run away from Egypt and work as a shepherd in the desert.

**Can you spot the mistake here?**
**Color the picture.**
**You can read this story**
**in Exodus 2:15–22 and 3:1.**

**27**

OCTOBER

Here is a picture of Jesus healing a man. Why is the man throwing away his stick?

Read this story in John 9:1–11 to find out.
Now color in the picture.

Color me!

# 9

## MARCH

One day, Moses saw a bush burning in the desert.

**Join up the dots to complete the picture.
You can read what happened when Moses saw
the bush in Exodus 3:1–14.**

DOT-TO-DOT

# 26

OCTOBER

Here are 6 pictures of the story about the loaves and fish — but they're in the wrong order.

**Number the pictures in the correct order and color them in. Read the story in John 6:1–15 to help you.**

Puzzle

**10**

MARCH

Moses and his brother Aaron were sent to tell Pharaoh to let their people go free.

**Color in this picture.**
**Read Exodus 5:1–9.**

Color me!

OCTOBER

Puzzle

When everybody has eaten enough, the disciples collect all the left-overs.

**How many full baskets are there?
Read John 6:13 to find out.
Which basket here is the odd one out?**

MARCH

*Talk to me!*

## What is Moses saying to Pharaoh, king of Egypt?

**Write in the speech bubble.**
**Read Exodus 5:1 to help you.**

# 24

## OCTOBER

Jesus' friends give the pieces of bread and fish to all the people.

**Color in this picture of everyone eating.
Read John 6:10–11.**

Color me!

**12**

MARCH

In Moses' time, God made dreadful things happen in Egypt. Once, thousands of frogs swarmed all over the land.

**Where are the frogs? Draw frogs everywhere, chasing the people. Read about this plague in Exodus 8:1–15.**

**Draw me!**

# 23
## OCTOBER

In this picture of the story of the loaves and fish, Jesus is breaking the bread before it is given to the people.

**Copy the picture into the blank box and then color it in.**
**What does Jesus do before he breaks the bread?**
**Read John 6:11 to find out.**

**Draw me!**

# 13
## MARCH

Another time, thousands of flies flew everywhere.

**Circle 10 differences between these 2 pictures.**
**Read about this plague in Exodus 8:20–30.**

SPOT THE DIFFERENCE

**22**

OCTOBER

The boy's picnic is 5 small loaves and 2 small fish.

The artist has drawn 4 outlines of fish. Which outline fits exactly the finished picture?
Read John 6:8–9.
Now complete all the fish and color them in.

Puzzle

**14**

MARCH

# God sent a terrible hailstorm on Egypt.

How many deliberate mistakes has the artist made here?
You can read this story in Exodus 9:13–35.

SPOT THE MISTAKE

# 21

## OCTOBER

### Search 👉

Jesus has been preaching all day and the people are hungry. A boy offers his picnic.

**Can you find all the bunches of grapes hidden in the picture?**
**Read John 6:5–13.**
**Was any food left after the picnic?**

**15**

MARCH

The cattle of Egypt all caught a terrible disease. But still Pharaoh wouldn't let the Hebrews go.

**Which 2 pictures are exactly the same?**
**You can find this story in Exodus 9:1–7.**

Puzzle

**20**

OCTOBER

Jesus is preaching here to a big crowd of people. But the artist hasn't drawn them.

**Can you add a crowd of people listening?**
**Read John 6:2.**

Draw me!

# 16
## MARCH

At last Pharaoh told Moses he could lead his people out of Egypt.

**Find all the funny mistakes the artist has made.**
**Read Exodus 12:31–33.**

SPOT THE MISTAKE

# 19
## OCTOBER

SPOT THE MISTAKE

Jesus is walking across the water to meet his disciples.

**How many funny mistakes can you find in the artist's drawing? Read Matthew 14:22–33.**

# 17
## MARCH

Before they left Egypt, the Hebrews had a special meal. They ate standing up and with their outdoor clothes on.

**Complete the second drawing of the man eating his Passover meal. Read God's instructions in Exodus 12:8–11.**

**Draw me!**

# 18

## OCTOBER

Zacchaeus has come down the tree to meet Jesus.

**Read the story again, then fill in his speech bubble. The story is in Luke 19:1–10.**

*Talk to me!*

# 18

MARCH

Finally Moses and his people left Egypt. They took all their belongings with them.

**How many cups can you find hidden in this picture?**
**Read Exodus 12:31–36.**

Search 👉

# 17

## OCTOBER

This little man climbed a tree to see Jesus.

**Read the story in Luke 19:1–10 and find out his name.**
**What sort of tree did he climb?**
**Now color in the picture.**

Color me!

# 19
## MARCH

## What is Moses doing here?

**Join up the dots to find out.**
**You can read this amazing escape story**
**in Exodus 14:1–29.**

DOT-TO-DOT

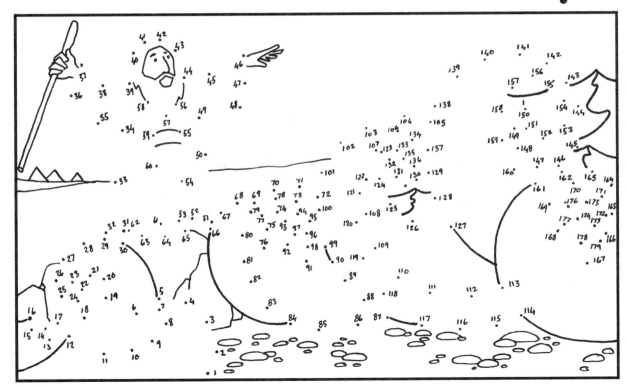

# 16
## OCTOBER

Here is another picture of the man Jesus healed while he was sitting beside the pool.

**Can you find all the crutches hidden in the drawing?**
**Read John 5:1–9.**

Search 👉

# 20
## MARCH

Can you help Moses and the Hebrews find their way to the palm trees at the oasis?

**You can read this story in your Bible in Exodus 15:22–27.**

maze

# 15

## OCTOBER

Here is another picture of a farmer sowing seed in his field.

Can you find 10 differences between these 2 pictures of the sower? Jesus explains the meaning of this story in Luke 8:11–15.

SPOT THE DIFFERENCE

**21**

MARCH

While the Hebrews were on the march, God led them with a pillar of fire during the night-time.

**Color in this picture of the Hebrews walking through the desert. Read Exodus 13:21–22.**

Color me!

# Jesus told a story about a farmer scattering his seeds.

**Join up the dots to find out what's happening here.**
**Read this story in Luke 8:4–8.**
**On how many different types of ground did the seed land?**

DOT-TO-DOT

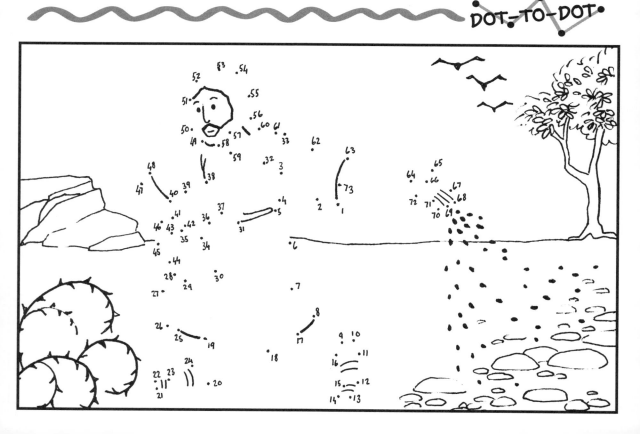

**22**

MARCH

Here are 6 pictures of the story of Moses. Can you number them so they are in the right order?

**Look in Exodus 2 – 14 to help you .**

Puzzle

# 13
## OCTOBER

SPOT THE MISTAKE

The disciples tried to keep these children away from Jesus, but he welcomed them.

**How many deliberate mistakes can you find in the picture? Read Luke 18:16.**

**23**

MARCH

The Hebrews complained that they were hungry in the desert, so God provided special food called manna.

**Can you find the bowls hidden here?**
**Read this story in Exodus 16:1–18.**

Search 👉

# 12

OCTOBER

Jesus told a story about a rich king who invited all sorts of people – even beggars and blind people – to come to a great party.

**Can you find 10 wine jars hidden here?**
**Read the complete story in Luke 14:15–24.**

Search

**24**

MARCH

Here is a picture of quails landing in the desert.

**Complete the picture by drawing the Israelite camp.**
**Read Exodus 16:1–13.**

Draw me!

**OCTOBER**

These 10 bridesmaids are waiting for the bridegroom. They each have a lamp.

**Which girl is the odd one out?**
**Read this story in Matthew 25:1–13.**

Puzzle

**25**

MARCH

Which of these two quails sent to feed the Hebrews are exactly the same? Look carefully!

**Read Exodus 16:11–13.**

Puzzle

# 10

## OCTOBER

*Talk to me!*

This man is building extra barns to store all his grain. What happens to him next?

**Read the story in Luke 12:16–21. Now fill in the speech bubble above the man's head.**

**26**

MARCH

God also provided the Hebrews with water from a rock.

**Can you find a funny mistake here?**
**Read Exodus 17:1–7.**

SPOT THE MISTAKE

**9**

OCTOBER

Here are 6 pictures of the Good Samaritan story, but they're in the wrong order.

**Number them in the order that they happened. You can read the story of the Good Samaritan in Luke 10:25–37.**

Puzzle

**27**

MARCH

Moses climbed Mount Sinai to meet God. He is carrying two stone tablets on which are written the Ten Commandments.

Copy this picture into the blank box and color it in.
Read about Moses' adventure in Exodus 19:16–19 and 24:12–13.

**Draw me!**

**8**

OCTOBER

The kind stranger who helped the man that had been robbed is often called the Good Samaritan.

**Follow the lines to find the way to the inn.**
**You can read this story in Luke 10:25–37.**

maze

**28**

MARCH

## Why does Moses look unhappy here?

**Read Exodus 32:1–20 and draw what Moses saw.**

**Draw me!**

## 7

### OCTOBER

Search 👉

A man who is a foreigner stops to help the man who has been robbed. He bandages him and takes him to an inn.

**How many jars of oil can you find hidden in the picture?**
**You can read the end of this story in Luke 10:33–37.**

**29**

MARCH

Moses was very angry when he came down Mount Sinai because the people were worshiping a golden idol. What did he **do?**

Read Exodus 32:19–20 to find out.
Can you spot the differences **between these two pictures?**

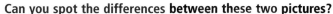

SPOT THE DIFFERENCE

# 6

## OCTOBER

A priest is passing the wounded traveler.
A helper in the Temple walks by.
Do they help?

**Can you find the funny mistakes that the artist has made?**
**You can find the answer to the question in Luke 10:31–32.**

SPOT THE MISTAKE

# 30

## MARCH

Join up the dots to see the idol the Hebrews were worshiping while Moses was on the mountain.

**Read Exodus 32:1–4.**

DOT-TO-DOT

**5**

OCTOBER

Join up the dots to find out who these men are hitting. Is it the traveler on his way to Jericho?

**Read Luke 10:30.**

DOT-TO-DOT

# 31
## MARCH

God wrote out the Ten Commandments on 2 new stone tablets.

**Which outline fits the finished picture?**
**Read Exodus 34:1–7 and 29.**

Puzzle

# 4

OCTOBER

Here is another story Jesus told. A man sets out on a journey from Jerusalem to Jericho.

**Help this man find the right way through the rocks.**

**You can read part 1 of this story in Luke 10:30.**

APRIL

Moses told the people he had instructions from God to make a big tent where the priests could sacrifice to God.

**Color in this picture of the tent, that is also called the Tabernacle. Read Exodus 25:1–9.**

Color me!

# 3
## OCTOBER

When the shepherd gets home with the lost sheep he calls his friends and neighbors.

**Read Luke 15:5–6.**
**Now fill in the shepherd's speech bubble.**

*Talk to me!*

# Here is another picture of the Tabernacle.

**Draw some priests in front of it and some tents of the Israelites in the background.**
**Now color it in.**
**Read Exodus 26:1–6.**

APRIL

**Draw me!**

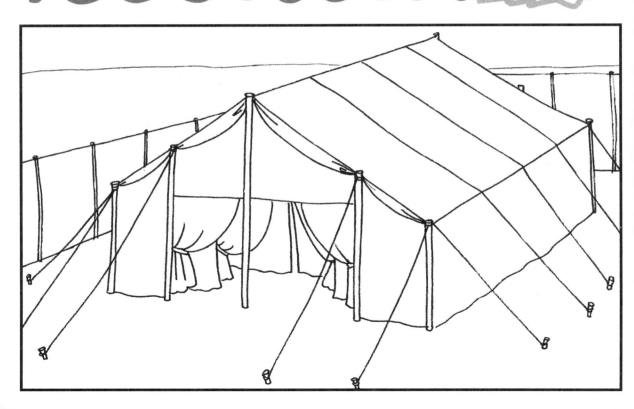

**OCTOBER**

# The shepherd carries his sheep home.

Here are some more sheep.
Which outline exactly fits the finished
drawing of the sheep?
Now finish all the drawings.
Read Luke 15:5–6.

*Puzzle*

**3**

APRIL

In the desert, the Israelites were bitten by poisonous snakes. Moses set up a bronze snake on a pole. If people looked at it, they were healed.

Spot the differences between these two pictures.
Read Numbers 21:4–9.

SPOT THE DIFFERENCE

OCTOBER

The shepherd is trying to reach the sheep that has strayed.

**Can you find the right way through the maze?**
**Read Luke 15:5–6.**
**Does the shepherd find his lost sheep?**

**4**

APRIL

Moses sent twelve men to spy out the Promised Land.

**Complete this drawing of the spies.**
**Read Numbers 13:1–2.**

**Draw me!**

# 30

SEPTEMBER

## One sheep is missing!

**Here are 7 of the shepherd's sheep.
Which is the odd one out?
Read Luke 15:4–5.**

SPOT THE DIFFERENCE

**5**

APRIL

Here is another picture of the twelve Israelite spies.

**Find the odd man out.**
**Read Numbers 13:17–20.**

Puzzle

# 29

## SEPTEMBER

It's the end of the day and the shepherd is counting his sheep. He should have 100.

**How many funny mistakes can you find here?**
**Read Luke 15:4–5.**

SPOT THE MISTAKE

**6**

**APRIL**

Ten of the spies came back from the Promised Land with frightening stories. They made all the people feel afraid.

Spot the differences between the pictures.

Read Numbers 13:21–32.

What did these 2 spies bring back with them?

SPOT THE DIFFERENCE

# 28

## SEPTEMBER

Here are 6 pictures of the boy who left home – but they're all mixed up.

**Number them in the right order.**
**Read the whole story in Luke 15:11–27 to help you.**

Puzzle

**7**

APRIL

But two of the spies said there was nothing to be afraid of. What did they say to the Israelites?

Read Numbers 14:5–9 to help you fill in the speech bubble.

*Talk to me!*

# 27

**SEPTEMBER**

The father is waiting for the son who left home.

**Finish the picture by drawing the son coming home.**
**Now color it in.**
**Read Luke 15:17–27.**

**Draw me!**

**8**

APRIL

Balaam and his donkey met an angel.
What did the angel say?

**Fill in the speech bubble.**
**Read this story in Numbers 22:21–35 to help you.**

*Talk to me!*

# 26

SEPTEMBER

The young man has run out of money. He's got a job feeding some very dirty pigs.

**Find the differences between these 2 pictures. Read Luke 15:14–16.**

SPOT THE DIFFERENCE

**9**

APRIL

The Israelites moved camp only when God told them to. The priests carried the Ark.

How many hidden bunches of grapes can you find in this picture?
Read Numbers 9:15–20.

Search

## Color me!

Here is the son who left home. He thinks he's having a great time. He's using all the money his father gave him.

**Color in the picture.**
**Read Luke 15:13.**

# 10

APRIL

Joshua was the new leader of the Israelites.

**Which 2 of these pictures are exactly the same?**
**Read Numbers 27:12–23.**

Puzzle

**24**

SEPTEMBER

Jesus told a story about a father with 2 sons. Here the father is waving goodbye to his younger son.

The artist hasn't finished the picture. Draw the son leaving. Now color in the picture.

Read the first part of the story in Luke 15:11–13.

**Draw me!**

**APRIL**

Old Moses never entered the Promised Land. Here he is looking towards it before he dies.

How many differences can you see between the 2 pictures? Read Deuteronomy 34:1–6.

SPOT THE DIFFERENCE

# 23

## SEPTEMBER

Jesus told many stories. In this story a woman is searching for her lost coin.

**The artist has hidden several coins.
How many can you find?
Read Luke 15:8–10.**

Search 👉

**12 APRIL**

At last Joshua led the Israelites out of the desert, across the River Jordan and into the Promised Land.

Find the deliberate mistakes in this picture of the priests carrying the Ark across the dry river bed.
Read this story in Joshua 3:1–17.

**22**

SEPTEMBER

Here is another picture of the man who Jesus healed after he'd been let down through the roof. What is he doing?

There are a lot of mistakes. Can you find them all?
Find the answer to the question in Luke 5:25.

SPOT THE MISTAKE

**13**

APRIL

## Color me!

There were strong walled cities in the Promised Land. What did God say to Joshua?

**Read God's promise to Joshua in Joshua 1:5–9.**
**Color this picture of Joshua.**

**21**

SEPTEMBER

Then Jesus said to the man,
"Pick up your mat and go home."

Can you find 13 keys hidden here?
Read Luke 5:25–26 to find out what happened next.

Search 👉

**14**

APRIL

Here is a Jewish priest with a ram's-horn trumpet, called a "shofar". They were used in battle.

Can you copy the artist's drawing? Now color it in.
Read Joshua 6:4.

Draw me!

## 20

SEPTEMBER

## Color me!

What did Jesus say to this man when he saw the faith of the 4 friends?

Read Luke 5:20 to find out.
Color in the picture carefully.

**15**

APRIL

The priests blew silver trumpets
to call the people to worship,
to war or to move camp.

**Find 2 pictures that are exactly the same.**
**Read Numbers 10:1–10.**

Puzzle

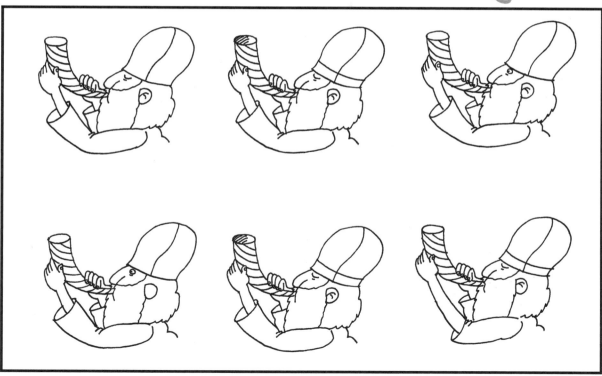

**19**

SEPTEMBER

One day 4 friends carried a man on a stretcher to a house where Jesus was teaching.

**Join up the dots.**
**Find out what is happening by reading Luke 5:17–19.**
**Now color in the picture .**

DOT-TO-DOT

# 16
## APRIL

Different trumpet calls
had different meanings.

**Complete the unfinished drawings of priests' trumpets.**
**Now color them all in brightly.**
**Read Numbers 10:1–10.**

**Draw me!**

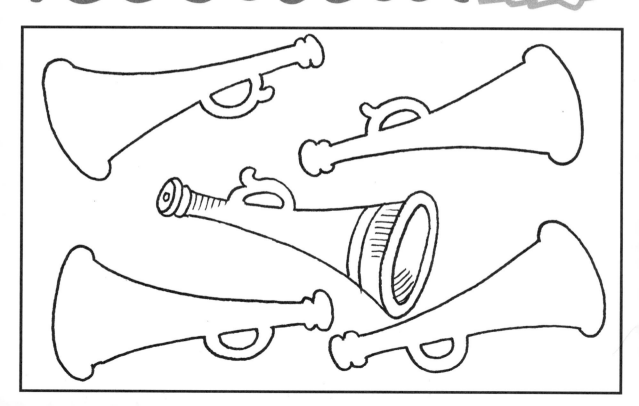

**18**

SEPTEMBER

The little girl's mother is bringing something for her to eat.

**Complete the drawing and color it in.**
**Read Luke 8:54–56.**

Draw me!

**17**

APRIL

Joshua sent Israelite spies into Jericho before he attacked. Here they are escaping from Rahab's house.

**Read this spy story in Joshua 2:1–16.**
**What happened to Rahab after Jericho fell?**
**Read Joshua 6:22–23.**

Color me!

**17**

SEPTEMBER

At Jairus' house everyone is crying because the little girl has died. What is Jesus saying to her?

**Read the story about the little girl in Luke 8:49–56. Now fill in Jesus' speech bubble.**

*Talk to me!*

## 18

APRIL

## Color me!

For six days the army marched around Jericho's walls. Each day they marched around once only, in silence. With them marched seven priests blowing trumpets.

**Color in this picture of the battle of Jericho.**
**Read Joshua 6:1–14.**

# 16

SEPTEMBER

SPOT THE MISTAKE

Why is this woman touching Jesus' cloak?

**Read Luke 8:41–48 to find out. How many silly mistakes can you find in the picture?**

# 19
## APRIL

On day seven, the army marched around seven times. The seventh time, the priests gave a signal and all the people shouted.

**Join up the dots to find out what happened when the war cry rang out. Read this story in Joshua 6:15–20.**

DOT-TO-DOT

# 15
## SEPTEMBER

Jairus has come to Jesus for help.

**Read Luke 8:40–42.**
**Now write in the speech bubble what Jairus is asking Jesus.**

*Talk to me!*

# 20

APRIL

Gideon was another brave leader of the Israelites. He chose his soldiers according to who drank the water with cupped hands.

**How many deliberate mistakes can you see here?**
**Read about Gideon's army in Judges 7:1–8.**

SPOT THE MISTAKE

# 14
## SEPTEMBER

Jesus is telling the storm to be still.
Are the disciples frightened?

**Read Mark 4:39–41 to find out.**
**How many bananas can you find hidden in the picture?**

Search

Here is Gideon selecting his soldiers. What is he saying to the men he hasn't chosen?

**Fill in his speech bubble. Read Judges 7:7–8 to help you. Gideon keeps only 300 men.**

*Talk to me!*

# 13

## SEPTEMBER

One day, Jesus was very tired,
and fell asleep in the boat.

**Join up the dots. What has happened on the Sea of Galilee?
To find the answer, read Mark 4:37–38.**

DOT-TO-DOT

**22**

APRIL

## Color me!

Gideon attacked the enemy using trumpets and torches!

**Color in this picture of the brave leader. Read all about it in Judges 7:16–22.**

# 12

## SEPTEMBER

Jesus often used his friends' boat to sail across the lake.

**Which outline fits the finished drawing of the boat? Read Mark 4:35–36.**

**23**

APRIL

Gideon used jars to conceal the soldiers' lights.

**Which two jars are exactly the same?**
**Read Judges 7:16.**

*Puzzle*

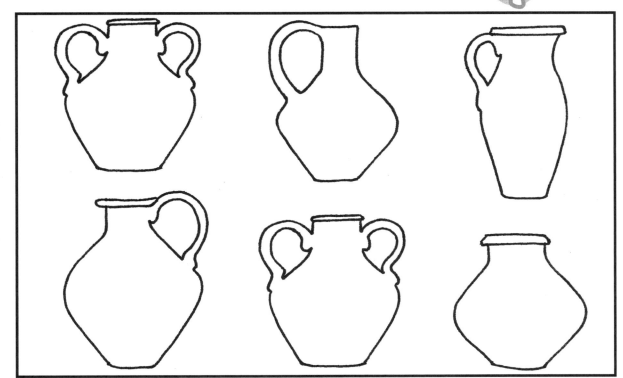

## SEPTEMBER

Jesus is preaching to the people from his friends' boat.

**Can you find the funny mistakes in the picture?**
**Read Mark 4:1 to find out why Jesus was in the boat.**

SPOT THE MISTAKE

**24**

APRIL

Deborah was another brave leader of the Israelites.

Can you find all the hidden daggers in this picture?
You can read about Deborah in Judges 4:4–16.

Search

# 10

SEPTEMBER

Jesus says to the lame man,
"Do you want to get well?"
And he heals him.

**Read the story in John 5:6–9 and color in the picture.**
**On which day of the week did Jesus heal the man?**

Color me!

# 25
APRIL

Strong man Samson carried off the city gates of Gaza.

**Can you finish the second picture of Samson carrying the huge door? Read this story in Judges 16:2–3.**

**Draw me!**

**9**

SEPTEMBER

This man can't move his legs. He's waiting at the pool to be made well.

Can you spot the differences between the 2 pictures?
Read about this man in John 5:1–5.
For how many years has he been ill?

SPOT THE DIFFERENCE

**26**

APRIL

Samson had a date with a young lady. When he was on his way to meet her, a lion attacked him.

**Join up the dots to find out what Samson is doing here. Read this story in your Bible in Judges 14:1–7.**

DOT-TO-DOT

**8**

SEPTEMBER

# The artist hasn't finished this picture.

**Read the story in John 12:1–3 then finish the picture.**
**What is the woman's name?**

**Draw me!**

# 27
## APRIL

Samson told his friend Delilah that if she tied up his arms while he was asleep he would lose his strength.

**Copy the picture into the blank box and color it in.**
**You can read this story in Judges 16:4–12.**

**Draw me!**

**7**

SEPTEMBER

John the Baptist has been thrown into prison by King Herod.

Copy the drawing into the empty box and then color it in.
Read Mark 6:17–18.

Draw me!

# 28

APRIL

Delilah discovered that Samson was only strong while his hair grew long. So she cut it short while he was asleep.

**How many differences are there between the 2 pictures?**
**Read the story in Judges 16:15–22.**

SPOT THE DIFFERENCE

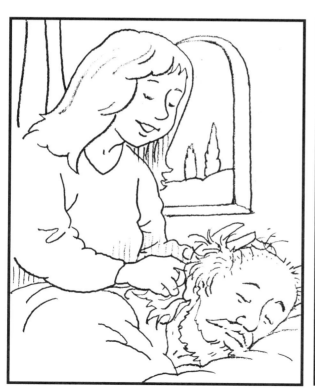

**6**

SEPTEMBER

A Roman soldier sent a message to Jesus which said, "My servant is ill. If you just give him a command, he will get better."

Join up the dots to complete the picture.
What did Jesus tell the people?
Read the story in Luke 7:1–10 to find out.

DOT-TO-DOT

29

APRIL

Samson was captured by his enemies. When his strength returned, he pulled down a building where they were having a party.

**Complete the picture of Samson at the party.**
**Read Judges 16:23–30 to help you.**

**Draw me!**

**5**

SEPTEMBER

# Jesus is teaching in the synagogue.

**Circle all the mistakes you can find.**
**How many do you have?**
**Read Mark 1:21–22.**

SPOT THE MISTAKE

# 30
APRIL

Here are 6 pictures of the story of Samson.
Number each box in the right order to
tell the story.

**Look in Judges 14 – 16 to help you.**

Puzzle

**SEPTEMBER**

*Talk to me!*

Matthew was a greedy
tax-collector, but Jesus
told Matthew to follow
him too.

**Read about the call of Matthew
in Matthew 9:9.
Fill in Jesus' speech bubble.**

**MAY**

Naomi's husband and two grown-up sons died in a foreign country. "I'm going back home," she said to her daughter-in-law, Ruth.

Complete the outline drawing of Naomi and Ruth.
Read this story in Ruth 1:1–15.

**Draw me!**

**3**

SEPTEMBER

In Jesus' story, the house built on sand falls down in the storm.

**Color the picture in.**
**Read Luke 6:49.**

Color me!

# What is Naomi saying to Ruth?

**Look in your Bible in Ruth 1:15 to help you fill in Naomi's speech bubble.**

*Talk to me!*

**2**

SEPTEMBER

Jesus told a story about 2 houses. This one is built on rock. It will stand firm.

**Draw in lightning and rain.**
**Read Luke 6:46–48.**

**Draw me!**

**3**

MAY

Ruth looked after her mother-in-law, Naomi, and went back to Bethlehem with her.

**Help Ruth find her way to Bethlehem and the wheatfields.**
**Read Ruth 1:16–22.**

*maze*

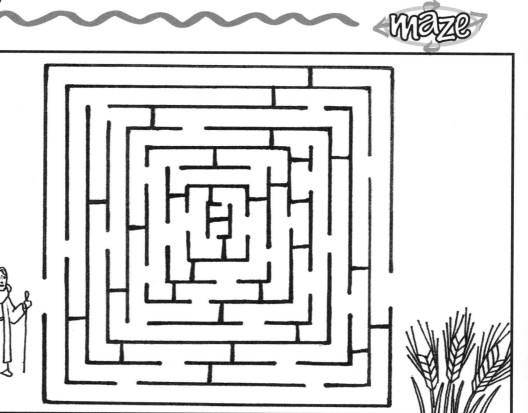

## SEPTEMBER

Jesus taught the people in the open-air. He said that God makes the flowers look more beautiful than even the richest king.

**Which is the odd one out?**
**Now color them in.**
**Read Jesus' words in Matthew 6:25–34.**

**4**

MAY

While she was living with Naomi in Bethlehem, Ruth went to gather grain in fields belonging to a man called Boaz.

**Join up the dots to find Ruth gathering grain.**
**Read about Ruth in the fields in Ruth 2.**

DOT-TO-DOT

## AUGUST 31

True or false? Jesus said we should do good deeds so that people will praise us.

Copy this picture into the blank box and color it in.
Read Matthew 5:14–16 to find out why we should do good things.

**Draw me!**

## 5 MAY

Boaz talked to Ruth while she was gathering grain. They grew to love each other, and got married.

**Find the funny mistakes in this picture.**
**Read Ruth 4:13–16. Why is Naomi very happy?**

SPOT THE MISTAKE

# 30

## AUGUST

## Jesus is preaching to the people.

Circle all the funny mistakes in the picture.
How many have you found?
Read Matthew 5:1–10 to find out what Jesus
is saying.

SPOT THE MISTAKE

**6**

MAY

One day a woman called Hannah came to the Tabernacle. She was sad because she had no children.

Copy the drawing into the blank box and color it in.
Read what Hannah prayed for in 1 Samuel 1:1–20.

**Draw me!**

# 29

## AUGUST

Jesus met a woman at a well in Samaria and asked her for water. He said he could give her everlasting water.

**Can you find any hidden buckets here?**
**Read this story in John 4:1–26.**

Search 👉

**7**

MAY

Hannah had a son called Samuel. She gave him to serve God in the Tabernacle.

Circle all the hidden coats in this picture.
Read about Hannah's promise in 1 Samuel 1:21 – 2:11.

Search 👉

# 28

## AUGUST

One night a man called Nicodemus visited Jesus.

**Find the deliberate mistakes in the picture.**
**Read what Nicodemus and Jesus**
**talked about in John 3:1–15.**

SPOT THE MISTAKE

**8**

MAY

# Samuel heard God call his name one night.

**Color in this picture of Samuel listening to God's voice.**
**Read this story in 1 Samuel 3:1–10.**

Color me!

# 27

## AUGUST

Jesus has told his friends
how to catch more fish.
Who does the boat belong to?

**Read this story in Luke 5:1–11 to find out.**
**Can you find the deliberate mistakes the artist has made?**

SPOT THE MISTAKE

# 9

MAY

One of Samuel's jobs each night was to light the lamp.

**The artist has drawn 7 pictures of the candlestick.**
**Which two are exactly the same?**
**Read 1 Samuel 3:2–3.**

Puzzle

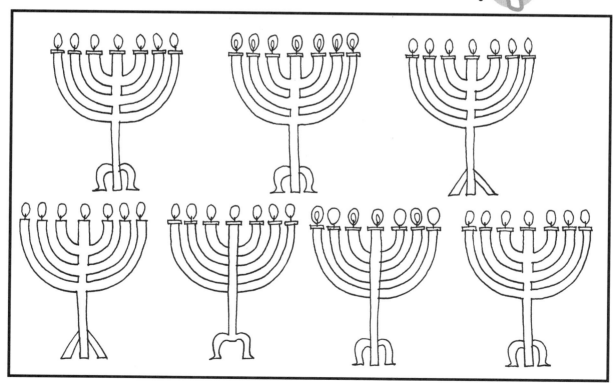

# 26
## AUGUST

Here is a picture of a good shepherd with his sheep.

**How many differences can you spot between the two pictures? Read John 10:14 to find out what Jesus called himself.**

SPOT THE DIFFERENCE

## 10 MAY

*Talk to me!*

Samuel is listening to God's voice.

**What did Samuel say to God?**
**Fill in the speech bubble.**
**Read 1 Samuel 3:8–10 to help you.**

**25**

AUGUST

When there was no more wine at the wedding, Jesus turned water into wine.

Here are 7 drawings of wine jars. Which is the odd one out?
Read the story of Jesus turning water into wine in John 2:1–11.

Puzzle

**11**

MAY

These enemies of Israel, called Philistines, are carrying off the Ark from the Tabernacle.

Finish off the picture and color it in. Look at the ark on the next page to help you.
Read 1 Samuel 4:17 and 5:1–3.

**Draw me!**

# 24

## AUGUST

Jesus did his very first miracle at a wedding in the village of Cana.

**Can you find 8 hidden wine jars?**
**Read this story in John 2:1–11.**

Search 👉

# 12
### MAY

Wherever the Ark was taken, people fell ill. After 7 months the Philistines sent it back.

**Which outline of the Ark of the Covenant matches the finished drawing?**
**Read 1 Samuel 5:6 and 6:1–2.**
**What are the winged creatures on top called?**
**Read Exodus 25:18 to find out.**

Puzzle

## 23 AUGUST

Join up the 3 men to the things linked with their work.

Follow the lines to discover the answers.

*maze*

MATTHEW

PAUL

PETER

# 13
## MAY

When Samuel grew up he became a prophet. He poured oil on Saul's head to show that Saul would be king of Israel.

**How many deliberate mistakes can you spot?**
**Read 1 Samuel 3:10–20 and 10:1.**

SPOT THE MISTAKE

# 22

AUGUST

## Jesus called 12 disciples.

**Can you find all the differences between the 2 pictures?**
**Find the names of all Jesus' disciples in Matthew 10:1–4.**

SPOT THE DIFFERENCE

**14**

MAY

Puzzle

David was a shepherd boy who looked after his father's flocks.

**Which 2 pictures are exactly the same? Read 1 Samuel 17:12–15.**

## 21
### AUGUST

SPOT THE MISTAKE

In this picture of Jesus calling James and John to follow him, the artist has made some mistakes.

Can you find all of the mistakes?
Read this story in Matthew 4:21–22.
Did they have televisions in Jesus' time?

**15**

MAY

The artist hasn't finished drawing these sheep: can you help?

Now color in the whole picture.
Read the "shepherd psalm", Psalm 23.

**Draw me!**

# What is Jesus saying to Peter and Andrew?

**Fill in the speech bubble with Jesus' words.**
**Read Matthew 4:18–20 to help you.**

*Talk to me!*

# 16

MAY

In the time of David, dangerous animals lived in the hills.

**David has met something that is trying to attack his flock of sheep.**
**Join up the dots to find out what it is.**
**You can read this story in 1 Samuel 17:34–37.**

DOT-TO-DOT

**19**

AUGUST

Peter and Andrew were fishermen when Jesus called them to follow him. They fished in the Sea of Galilee.

**Can you find 10 fish hiding in this picture?**
**Read this story in Matthew 4:18–20.**

Search

## MAY 17

## Color me!

The prophet Samuel poured oil on David's head to show that one day he would be king of Israel.

**Color in this picture of David being anointed with oil.**
**Read this story in 1 Samuel 16:1–13.**

**18**

AUGUST

After his baptism, Jesus was tempted by Satan.

**Find the differences between the 2 pictures.
Read Matthew 4:1–11.**

SPOT THE DIFFERENCE

**18**

MAY

David is taking some food to his brothers, who are fighting for the king.

Can you find the apples hidden in the picture?
Read 1 Samuel 17:17–21.

Search 👉

# 17
## AUGUST

As Jesus came out of the water,
God's voice spoke from heaven.

**Join up the dots to complete the picture.**
**Read Matthew 3:17 to discover what God said.**

DOT-TO-DOT

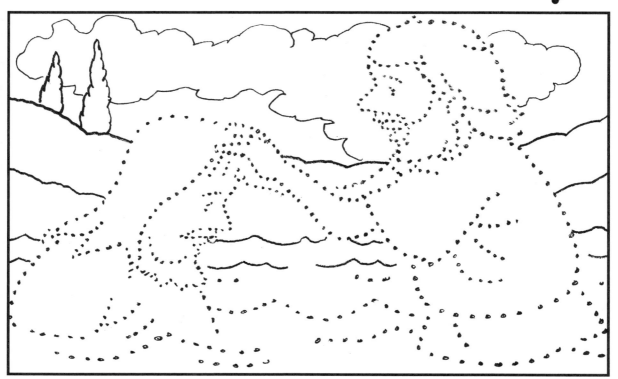

**19**

MAY

David said he wanted to fight the giant Goliath, and Saul offered to lend him his armor.

**Copy this picture into the blank box and color it in. Read 1 Samuel 17:20–40.**

**Draw me!**

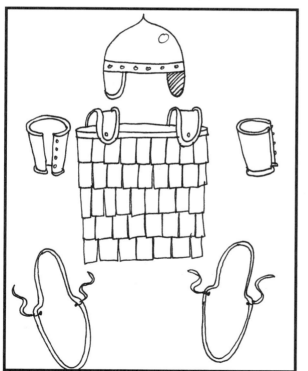

**16**

AUGUST

Jesus went to see John the Baptist. He asked John to baptise him in the River Jordan.

**Find the funny mistakes here.**
**Read Matthew 3:13–15.**

SPOT THE MISTAKE

## 20 MAY

Puzzle

The giant Goliath had a huge sword.

**Which 2 of these 5 swords are exactly the same?**
**Read 1 Samuel 17:4–7 and 45.**

**15**

**AUGUST**

Jesus said to Mary, "Didn't you know I had to be in my Father's house?"

Can you find the scrolls that are hidden in this picture of the Temple?
Now color in the picture.
Read how this story ends in Luke 2:49–52.

Search

**21**

MAY

David collects 5 stones from the stream and puts them in his bag. What is he saying to Goliath?

**Write your answer in the speech bubble.**
**Read 1 Samuel 17:40 and 45–47 to help you.**

*Talk to me!*

# 14

## AUGUST

### At last Mary and Joseph found Jesus with the priests.

**Can you find 8 fish hidden in this picture?**
**Read part 3 of this story in Luke 2:45–48.**
**What is Mary saying to Jesus?**

Search

# 22
MAY

David puts a stone in his sling.
He swings the sling in the air.

**The artist has made lots of silly mistakes
in this picture of David and Goliath.
How many can you find?
Check the story in 1 Samuel 17 if you're not sure.**

SPOT THE MISTAKE

**13**

**AUGUST**

Jesus spent time in the Temple talking to the priests. Mary and Joseph were looking for him everywhere.

**Can you find 10 differences between these 2 pictures?**
**Read part 2 of this story in Luke 2:43–45.**

SPOT THE DIFFERENCE

**23** MAY

The stone from the sling hits Goliath.
What happens next?

Read 1 Samuel 17:48–50 to find out.
Complete the outline drawing of Goliath.

**Draw me!**

When Jesus was twelve, he visited Jerusalem with Joseph and Mary.

**Color in this picture of them on their journey.**
**Read part 1 of this story in Luke 2:41–42.**

Color me!

**24**

MAY

Puzzle

David played the harp, or lyre. He also made up songs.

**Which outline fits the finished drawing of a harp?**

**You can read about David's harp in 1 Samuel 16:18.**

**Psalm 8 is one of David's songs.**

AUGUST

Here are Joseph, Mary and baby Jesus on their way to Egypt.

**Use the outline to help you copy the artist's picture.**
**Read Matthew 2:13–15.**

**Draw me!**

**25**
MAY

King Saul's servants said to David's father,
"The king needs your son, David."

Here is a drawing of a different harp. Which outline matches the
finished picture?
Read 1 Samuel 16:20 to find out what else David took with him.

Puzzle

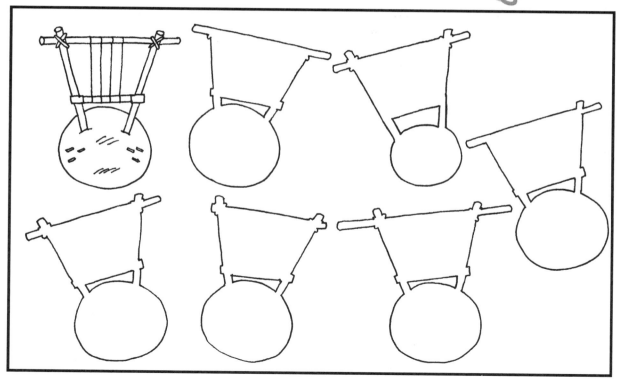

# 10

## AUGUST

An angel told Joseph it wasn't safe to stay in Bethlehem, so he took Mary and baby Jesus to Egypt.

**Join up the dots to complete the picture.**
**Read Matthew 2:13–15.**

DOT-TO-DOT

# What is David doing here in front of King Saul?

**Join up the dots to find out.**
**Read the story in 1 Samuel 16:14–23.**

MAY

DOT-TO-DOT

**9**

AUGUST

Simeon was an old man when he saw baby Jesus. He was very happy because he had been waiting for Jesus to be born.

**Can you find the mistakes in the picture?**
**Read about Simeon in Luke 2:21–35.**

SPOT THE MISTAKE

**27**

MAY

When David played his harp,
King Saul felt happy.

How many differences can you spot between these 2 pictures?
Read 1 Samuel 16:21–23.

SPOT THE DIFFERENCE

## AUGUST

Why do the 3 wise men <u>not</u> return to Herod?

**Read Matthew 2:12 to find the answer.
Here are 3 pictures of the wise men's gifts for Jesus.
Which picture is the odd one out?**

# 28

**MAY**

Everyone liked David, and Saul became more and more jealous. One day Saul hurled a spear at David.

**Draw David with his harp ducking to avoid the spear.**
**This story is in 1 Samuel 19:9–10.**

**Draw me!**

**7**

AUGUST

The wise men each brought a present for baby Jesus.

**Color in this picture of them with baby Jesus.**
**Read Matthew 2:11 to find out what gifts they brought to him.**

Color me!

**29**

MAY

David's friend Jonathan, who was Saul's son, fired an arrow in the air to warn David that he was in danger.

Copy the picture into the blank box and color it in.
Read 1 Samuel 20:32–42.

**Draw me!**

**6**

AUGUST

The wise men saw the star again and followed it to find the newborn baby. It stopped right over the place where Jesus was born.

**Can you find 10 differences between these 2 pictures of Bethlehem? Read the next part of the wise men's story in Matthew 2:9–10.**

SPOT THE DIFFERENCE

# 30

MAY

One night, David discovered King Saul asleep. David had his chance to kill Saul.

**How many deliberate mistakes has the artist made in this picture?**
**Read this story in 1 Samuel 26:7–12.**
**What did David do?**

SPOT THE MISTAKE

# 5

## AUGUST

*Talk to me!*

The wise men visited King Herod and asked him if he knew where they could find the newborn king.

**Read Matthew 2:1–8.**
**What is Herod saying to the wise men?**
**Fill in the speech bubble.**
**Do you believe Herod when he says he wants to worship Jesus?**

MAY

David is running away from Saul to a cave in the desert.

**Can you help him find his way to the cave?**
**Read 1 Samuel 23:14 to find out who kept David safe.**

**4**

AUGUST

In this picture of the wise men seeking Jesus, the artist has hidden some stars.

**How many can you find?**
**Read Matthew 2:1–2.**

Search 👉

**1**

JUNE

King Saul was killed in battle and David was crowned king of all Israel.

Copy this drawing into the blank box and color it in. Read 2 Samuel 5:1–4.

**Draw me!**

# 3

AUGUST

What are the wise men looking at in this picture?

**Join up the dots to find out.**
**Read Matthew 2:1–2.**

DOT-TO-DOT

# 2

JUNE

Here are 6 crowns. Which crown is the odd one out?

**Read 2 Samuel 5:3–4.**

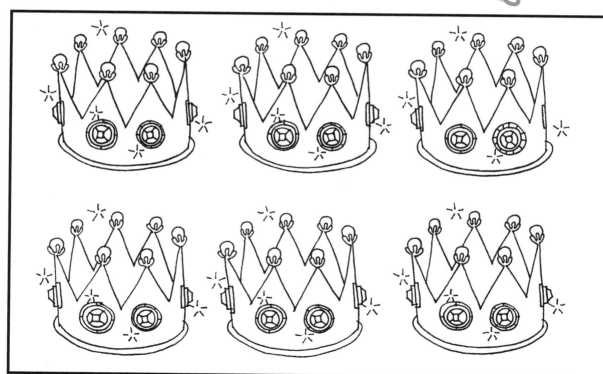

**2**

AUGUST

In this picture of the shepherds visiting the stable, the artist has deliberately made some silly mistakes.

**Circle all the mistakes you can find. How many have you spotted? Read the story in Luke 2:15–20.**

SPOT THE MISTAKE

**3**

JUNE

King David captured the city of Jerusalem and made it his capital.

**How many swords can you find hidden here?**
**Read 2 Samuel 5:6–9.**

Search 👉

AUGUST

These shepherds look surprised in this picture.

**Read Luke 2:8–14 to find out why.**
**Use these verses to help you fill in the angel's speech bubble.**

*Talk to me!*

**4**

JUNE

When David became king, he ordered the priests to bring the Ark to Jerusalem.

Join up the dots to find out what pulled the cart part of the way to Jerusalem.

Read about David dancing and singing in 2 Samuel 6:12–15.

DOT-TO-DOT

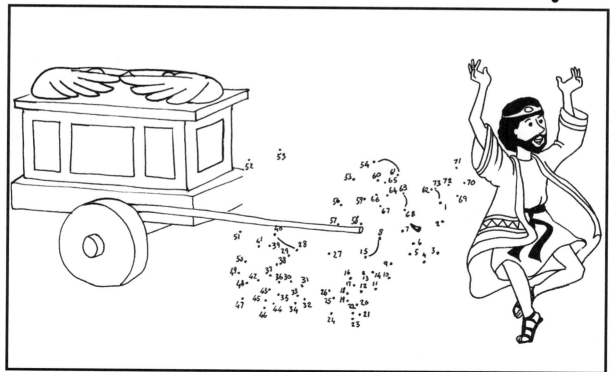

**31**

JULY

Here are 6 pictures of the story of the birth of Jesus.

**Number them in the right order.**
**Look in Luke 1 – 2 to help you.**

Puzzle

# 5

JUNE

Here are 6 pictures from the story of David.

**Number them in the right order.**
**Look in 1 Samuel 16 – 17 and 2 Samuel 5 – 6 to help you.**

Puzzle

# 30

## JULY

## Color me!

Joseph and Mary have just arrived at the inn at Bethlehem. What is the innkeeper's wife saying?

Read Luke 2:1–7.
Now color in the picture.

**JUNE**

## Color me!

King Solomon was very famous because he was so wise. People came from near and far to listen to his words.

**Color in this picture of Solomon on his throne.**
**Read 1 Kings 4:29–34.**

# 29
## JULY

It was nearly time for Jesus to be born. But Mary and Joseph had to go on a long journey.

**Help them find the right road.**
**You can read this story in Luke 2:1–5.**
**What is the name of the place where they are going?**

maze

**7**

JUNE

Two women are arguing about who this baby belongs to. They ask Solomon to decide.

**Join up the dots to complete the picture.**
**Read 1 Kings 3:17–23.**

DOT-TO-DOT

# 28

JULY

At last Elizabeth's son was born. His father couldn't speak, so he wrote the baby's name. It was "John".

**Can you find the deliberate mistakes in the picture? Read Luke 1:57–66.**

SPOT THE MISTAKE

# How does Solomon discover the true mother?

**Fill in his speech bubble.**
**Read 1 Kings 3:24–28 to help you.**

*Talk to me!*

**27**

JULY

**Puzzle**

One day Joseph will teach Jesus how to be a carpenter.

**Here are some carpenter's tools. Which is the odd one out? Read Mark 6:3.**

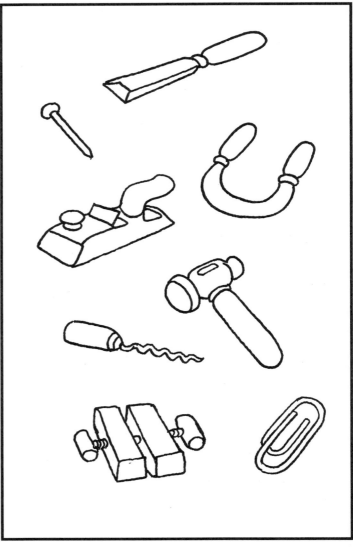

**9**

JUNE

The Queen of Sheba came a long way to visit King Solomon because she had heard that he was very wise.

**How many differences can you see between the 2 pictures? Read this story in 1 Kings 10:1–13.**

SPOT THE DIFFERENCE

# 26

JULY

## Joseph was a carpenter.

**Can you find 10 differences between these 2 pictures of Joseph hammering in his workshop? Read Matthew 13:55.**

SPOT THE DIFFERENCE

# 10

## JUNE

King Solomon built a magnificent Temple in Jerusalem.

**How many funny mistakes can you find in this picture?**
**Read about the building of the Temple in 2 Chronicles 3.**

SPOT THE MISTAKE

**25**

JULY

Joseph was engaged to Mary. An angel told him in a dream that Mary would have a special baby boy.

**How many rings can you find hidden here?**
**Read Matthew 1:18–25.**

Search

JUNE

The artist hasn't finished this picture of Solomon's Temple.

**Complete it for him, with priests coming and going, then color it in. Read 2 Chronicles 3.**

**Draw me!**

**24**

JULY

Mary had a cousin named Elizabeth, who was also expecting a baby boy.

**Join up the dots to complete the picture.**
**Read Luke 1:36, 39–42.**

DOT-TO-DOT

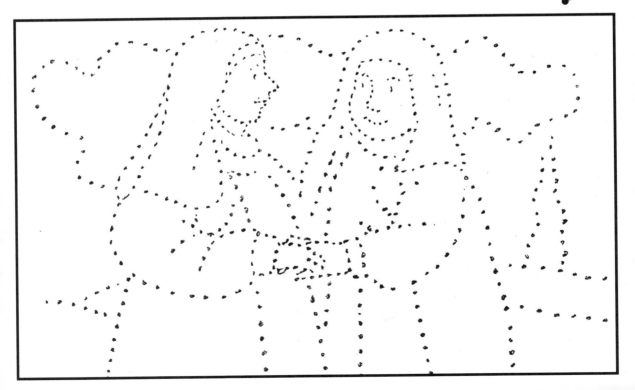

# 12

## JUNE

Here are six pictures from the story of King Solomon.

**Can you number them in the right order?**
**Look in 1 Kings 1 – 6 to help you.**

Puzzle

**23 JULY**

Mary lived in the little town of Nazareth.
One day she had an unexpected visitor.

**Can you find the deliberate mistakes in the picture?**
**You can read this story in Luke 1:26–38.**

SPOT THE MISTAKE

## JUNE

There was a famine and the prophet Elijah was alone and very hungry.

Join up the dots to find out how he received food.
Read this story in 1 Kings 17:1–6.

## 22

JULY

Here is Jonah telling the people of Nineveh that God will punish them.

Copy the picture into the blank box and color it in.
Read Jonah 3:4–10.
What did the people do – and what did God do?

**Draw me!**

**14**

JUNE

## Puzzle

Here are four ravens.
Which is the odd one out?

**Read about Elijah and the ravens
in 1 Kings 17:1–6.**

**JULY**

Finally, Jonah set off for Nineveh as he had been told.

**Can you help Jonah find the right route? Read Jonah 3:1–3.**

**15**

JUNE

God told Elijah to stay with a poor widow who had no food. While he stayed with the widow, her jug of olive oil and jar of flour never ran out.

Color in this picture of the widow pouring oil from her jug.
Read 1 Kings 17:7–16.

Color me!

**20**

JULY

Here is the huge fish that swallowed Jonah.

**Which outline matches exactly the finished picture?**
**Read Jonah 2:10.**
**Why did the fish swim to land?**

Puzzle

**16**

JUNE

Elijah built a stone altar and put wood on it, and an ox for a sacrifice. Then he poured lots of jarfuls of water over it.

**Which outline fits the finished water jar?**
**Read 1 Kings 18:30–35.**

Puzzle

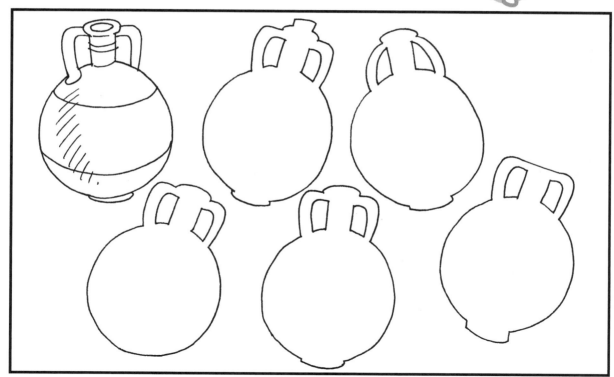

# 19
JULY

The fish spat Jonah out.
What is Jonah saying?

**Fill in Jonah's speech bubble.**
**Read Jonah 2:1–10 to help you.**

*Talk to me!*

# 17

JUNE

## Elijah prayed to God.

**Join the dots to discover what happened next.**
**Read 1 Kings 18:36–39.**
**All the people knew that Elijah's God was the true God.**

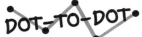

DOT-TO-DOT

**18**

JULY

# The huge fish is about to swallow Jonah.

Copy this picture into the blank box and color it in.
Read Jonah 1:17, 2:1.

**Draw me!**

# 18

JUNE

Elijah has fled to the desert to get away from wicked Queen Jezebel.

**Can you help him find his way across the desert?**
**Read the story in 1 Kings 19:1–9.**

maze

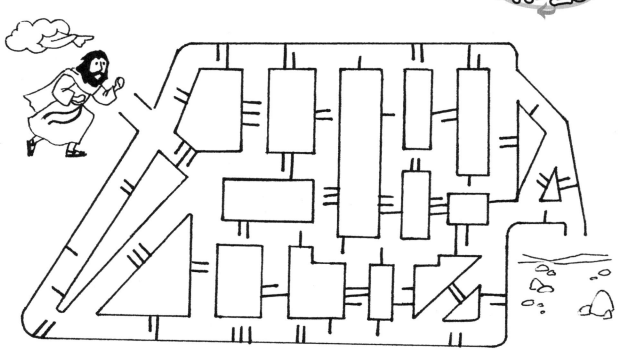

**JULY**

Jonah was thrown into the sea after a terrible storm hit the ship he was in.

Join up the dots to complete the picture.
You can read this story in Jonah 1:3–16.

DOT-TO-DOT

**JUNE**

SPOT THE MISTAKE

King Ahab decided that he wanted to have a vineyard that belonged to a man called Naboth.

**How many funny mistakes are in this picture?**
**Read this story in 1 Kings 21.**

**16** JULY

God told Jonah to go and preach in Nineveh.

**Can you find the mistakes here?**
**What did Jonah do?**
**Read Jonah 1:1–3.**

**20**

JUNE

What happened to Elijah when he finished his life on earth?

Read about Elijah and Elisha in 2 Kings 2:1–13.
Then color in this picture.

Color me!

**15**

JULY

# Shadrach, Meshach and Abednego are all in a blazing furnace.

**Use the outline the artist has given you to copy his picture.**
**Read the whole story in Daniel 3:1–30.**

**Draw me!**

# Elijah left behind his cloak for Elisha.

**How many differences can you find between these two pictures of Elisha looking at Elijah's cloak? Read 2 Kings 2:13–14.**

SPOT THE DIFFERENCE

# 14

JULY

Here are 6 pictures from the story of Daniel – but they're in the wrong order.

**Number them in the right order.**
**Look in Daniel 5 – 6 to help you.**

Puzzle

**22**

JUNE

Naaman had a terrible skin disease.
His wife had good news for him.

Find the candles hidden in the picture.
Read about Naaman in 2 Kings 5:1–3.

Search 👉

**13**

JULY

King Darius was pleased that the lions' mouths were shut and that Daniel was kept safe in the den of lions.

**Color in this picture.**
**Read this story in Daniel 6:19–23.**

Color me!

# 23

JUNE

Naaman's slave girl is telling him where to go to be healed.

**Write what the servant girl is saying in her speech bubble. Read 2 Kings 5:2–5 to help you.**

*Talk to me!*

JULY

Daniel was thrown
into a den of lions.

**Which is the odd one out here?**
**Read this story in Daniel 6:6–18.**

# 24

JUNE

Naaman is setting out to meet Elisha to see if Elisha can help him.

**Can you show Naaman the way?**
**Read 2 Kings 5:4–7.**

JULY

The prophet Daniel looks a bit worried.

**Read Daniel 6:5–18 to find out why.**
**Now complete the picture.**

Draw me!

**25**

JUNE

Naaman is dipping in the River Jordan as Elisha told him to do.

**How many times does he dip himself before he is clean?**
**Read 2 Kings 5:8–14 to find out.**
**Now color the picture.**

Color me!

**10**

JULY

The king forbade anyone to pray to God —
but Daniel's enemies spied on him praying.

**Find 10 bones hidden in the picture.**
**Read Daniel 6:6–11.**

Search

**26**

JUNE

Elisha helped some young men find an axe-head that had fallen into the river.

**How many funny mistakes has the artist put into this picture?**
**Read this story in 2 Kings 6:1–7.**

SPOT THE MISTAKE

# 9

JULY

At a great banquet the king of Babylon was terrified when he saw a hand write a warning on the wall.

**How many differences are there between these 2 arms? You can read the warning in Daniel 5:25–28.**

SPOT THE DIFFERENCE

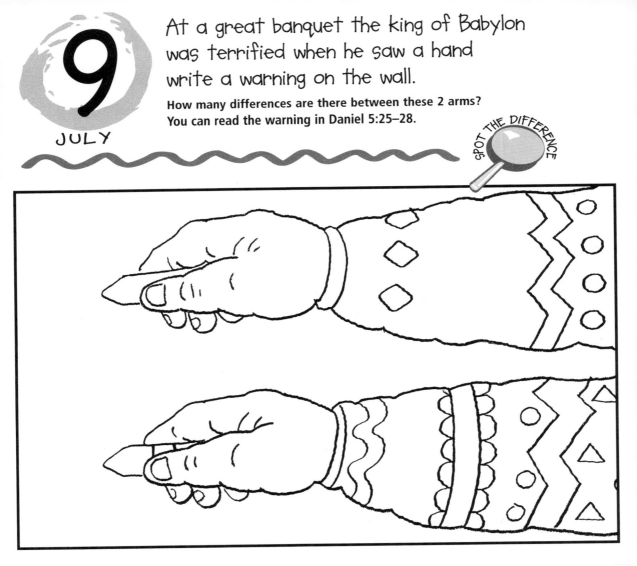

JUNE

Puzzle

Here are five axes.

**Can you find just two that are exactly alike?**
**Read 2 Kings 6:1–7.**

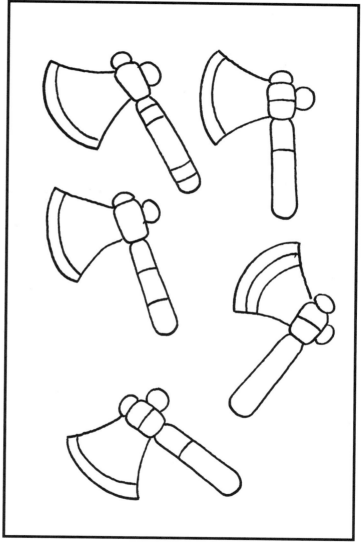

**8**

JULY

When he was in Babylon Daniel refused rich food and wine and only ate vegetables and drank water.

Copy the picture into the empty box and color it in.
Read Daniel 1:3–16.

**Draw me!**

## 28

JUNE

King Hezekiah is praying to God to help him reign as a good king.

**Copy this drawing into the empty box and then color it in. Read 2 Kings 18:1–8.**

**Draw me!**

# 7

JULY

Queen Esther saved her people from a terrible disaster. Here she is bowing to someone.

**Join up the dots to see who it is.**
**The answer is in Esther 5:1–2.**

DOT-TO-DOT

**29**

JUNE

King Josiah is repairing God's Temple in Jerusalem.

How many cups can you find hidden in the picture?
Read 2 Kings 22:1–7.

Search

**JULY**

Because the Israelites kept doing wrong, they were taken captive to Babylon.

**Find the way from Israel to Babylon. Read 2 Kings 25:8–12.**

# 30

JUNE

The high priest found a scroll of the Law in the Temple. It had been lost for many years.

**Which scroll here is the odd one out?**
**Read 2 Kings 22:8.**

Puzzle

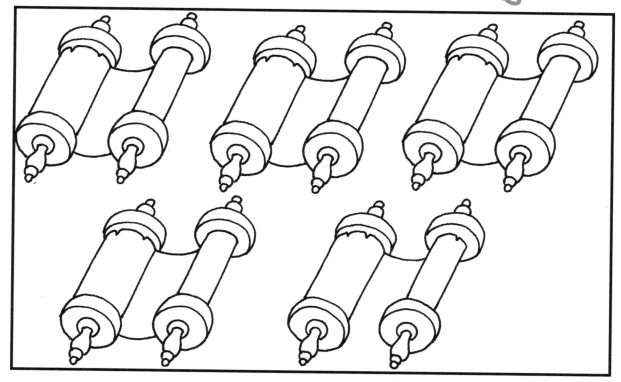

**5**

JULY

The Assyrians attacked Jerusalem and took precious treasures from the Temple itself.

Circle all the silly mistakes in this picture of the enemy carrying off goods from the Temple.
Read 2 Kings 24:10–14.

SPOT THE MISTAKE

JULY

DOT-TO-DOT

The high priest told the secretary and the secretary told the king. The king told all the people.

**What is this picture? Join up the dots to find out, then color it in.**
**Read 2 Kings 22:8–10 and 23:1–3.**

**4**

JULY

Jeremiah the prophet was thrown into a dirty pit because people didn't like what he was saying.

**Complete this picture by drawing a rope and people pulling Jeremiah out.**
**Read Jeremiah 38:4–13.**

**Draw me!**

**2** JULY

Job was a very rich and good man.
All he had was taken from him,
but he still trusted God.

**Copy this drawing into the blank box and color it in.
Read Job 19:25.**

**Draw me!**

**3**

JULY

The prophet Isaiah brought many messages from God. He said that one day a Savior would come like a bright light.

**How many oil lamps can you find hidden in this picture?**
**Read Isaiah 60:1–3.**

Search